SCREWTAPE LETTERS STUDY GUIDE

A Bible Study on the
C.S. Lewis Book The Screwtape Letters

By Alan Vermilye

Our cause is never more in danger than when a human, no longer desiring, but still intending, to do our Enemy's will, looks round upon a universe from which every trace of Him seems to have vanished, and asks why he has been forsaken, and still obeys.

Screwtape
The Screwtape Letters

Screwtape Letters Study Guide
A Bible Study on the C.S. Lewis Book
The Screwtape Letters

ISBN: 1512207292
ISBN-13: 978-1512207293

To learn more about this Bible study, order additional copies, or to download the answer guide visit.**www.ScrewtapeLettersStudyGuide.com**

Scripture quotations taken from the New American Standard Bible®, Copyright © 1960, 1962, 1963, 1968, 1971, 1972, 1973, 1975, 1977, 1995 by The Lockman Foundation Used by permission.
(www.Lockman.org)

Version 1

Table of Contents

ACKNOWLEDGMENTS

I would like to thank Jesus Christ for inspiring me each day to continue learning and growing in Him, my beautiful wife Sherry for listening to me wax on about this book as well as editing it for me, my kids Zane, Maddie, Olivia and Emma, Steve Urban for providing an excellent foreword to the study, my study group who served as guinea pigs for this study, and obviously C.S. Lewis for writing such an excellent book.

Foreword

In advising how to keep his *patient's* life with God ineffective and arbitrary, a senior devil admonishes a junior to, "Keep his mind on the inner life . . . For if he ever comes to make the distinction, if ever he consciously directs his prayers 'Not to what I think thou art but to what thou knowest thyself to be', our situation is . . . desperate." And so C.S. Lewis launches us into a collection of devilish letters from Uncle Screwtape to his "nephew" Wormwood in his classic and widely popular, *The Screwtape Letters*.

Lewis wrote about the inspiration for the book in a letter to his brother who had recently been rescued from Nazi-surrounded Dunkirk during WWII. Lewis explained that in church on July 21, 1940—the morning after he had listened to a very persuasive radio speech by Hitler that made even Lewis wavier in his convictions—he had been "struck by an idea for a book which I think might be both useful and entertaining. It would be called *As One Devil to Another* . . . The idea would be to give all the psychology of temptation from the *other* point of view."

As much as *The Screwtape Letters* did indeed prove to be very 'useful' to thousands during the confusion of WWII, it is a book equally valuable for us in today's culture of rapid change and confusion. Recognizing an enemy of truth and the Christian faith in the complex world around us is challenging, yet recognizing the subtle, shadowy whispers and twists of an enemy within is often even more difficult. But before there can be hope of progress in dealing with any enemy, that enemy must first be recognizable. Therefore any assistance and wisdom in this recognition is genuinely welcomed. And this what Alan Vermilye has done with his study of Lewis's *The Screwtape Letters*.

Vermilye walks the reader through each Screwtape letter and wisely asks questions to bring out turns and twists in the thoughts and emotions that we each experience and that Lewis wanted us to recognize. He helps us to see where crippling "truths" are often nothing more than half-truths and lies that enslave us with pride and defensiveness or shame and reticence.

From his years of teaching Bible study classes, Vermilye also smartly adds Scripture to weigh in on the discussion. For anyone or group that wants to become more intimate with God by re-assessing some of the enemies strongholds within, I highly recommend Alan Vermilye's study.

Steven Urban PhD

Double-board certified Physiatric Interventional Pain Specialist

Author of *Mere Christianity Study Guide: A Bible Study on the C.S. Lewis Book Mere Christianity*

INTRODUCTION

For some time I wanted to read *The Screwtape Letters*. I would start, and then, for whatever reason, stop. Let's face it: some of Lewis' writings can be an intellectual exercise that require dedication to seeing them through. I would say this is especially true for me. However, having read his *Mere Christianity* several times and completing the *Mere Christianity Study Guide* by Steve Urban twice, I felt I was finally up to the challenge.

I committed myself to both reading the book and creating a Bible study guide for it. Recognizing the daunting task before me, I decided to lead the study at my own church while writing it. I knew this would help develop the study and provide the accountability I would desperately need to see it through.

The Screwtape Letters is not a very long book. There are 31 letters that are only five pages each and at the most six paragraphs. I began with research and found some insightful posts, commentaries, and a few discussion questions to help prime the pump. I also kept Google handy since Lewis was a very articulate man with a vast vocabulary.

Creating a Bible study around the content seemed to flow effortlessly. Obviously Lewis already provided excellent content; I simply had to draw parallels with various Scripture passages to help us relate to the main theme of each letter. I have also included answers for each question that are available at www.ScrewtapeLettersStudyGuide.com.

Facilitating group discussion at my church was probably the most valuable part of the experience. Not only did it help better refine the study, but I also learned from each class member as they shared their interpretation of what they read. I'm eternally grateful for their participation and input on the study.

I'm not a biblical or Lewis scholar nor do I consider this study guide the most comprehensive work available on the book. However, it has helped me and others in my class come to a better understanding of Lewis' great classic. I hope it does for you as well.

BOOK SUMMARY

Our cause is never more in danger than when a human, no longer desiring, but still intending, to do our Enemy's will, looks round upon a universe from which every trace of Him seems to have vanished, and asks why he has been forsaken, and still obeys. - Screwtape

Why do we sometimes succeed spiritually, and at other times we fail? Are there a host of spiritual forces battling to influence the choices we make, or are we left to our own devices?

The Screwtape Letters by C.S. Lewis provides unique insight into the battles that are being waged in the spiritual world. The story is told through a collection of letters from Screwtape, an undersecretary in the lowerarchy of Hell, to his incompetent nephew, Wormwood. Wormwood is a junior devil who has just been given his first human, a young man (referred to as the patient), to corrupt and secure for eternity.

The story takes place in England during the tumultuous years of World War II with the man contemplating Christianity. However, another setting could very easily be his consciousness where another war is taking place for his soul. Each letter is filled with detailed instructions from Screwtape to Wormwood on how to best enter the man's thoughts and subtly influence his choices thereby guiding him closer to Hell.

There is nothing extraordinary about this man's life, but from the moment of contemplating faith until his last breath, he undergoes spiritual attack. Like most young adults, he is influenced by culture, materialistic friends, and the media. Each provides excellent distractions from his spiritual journey, but his quest for spiritual truth wins out, and eventually he becomes a Christian.

Early on, he struggles with balancing the unrealistic expectations of being an ideal Christian with what he encounters in the world, the church, his family, and daily life. The strange habits and hypocrisies of fellow church members and the prospect of his own mother doubting his new-found faith were unexpected, but they did not discourage him.

Building a dedicated prayer life becomes one of his top priorities. Battling everyday distractions, he quickly learns that being completely transparent with God is hard but also refreshing.

Living during a time of war, the man knows it's only a matter of time before he must make a stand. What is the Christian response to war? Should he take up arms and fight for his country against an evil tyrant, or should he refuse on moral grounds? He decides in favor of military service and now must learn to control his fear and hatred of a distant enemy whom he has never met.

As with life, the Christian journey is filled with mountain-top and valley experiences. Various trials and temptations common to all men come his way. He resolves to rise above each and finds himself strengthened with a renewed sense of self along the way.

He soon becomes aware that building relationships in a world hostile to his faith is difficult. He knows that he is to be in the world but not of the world. As a result he must distance himself from the negative influences in his life while maintaining relationships that he can either positively influence or be encouraged by.

Overtime with the busyness and noise of everyday life, he finds himself drifting away from his faith. It's so gradual at first that he does not notice he's slipping back into old habits. He's quickly awakened from his spiritual drift by experiencing real, simple pleasures that allow him to recover and recommit fully to his faith.

This experience has a dramatic impact on his life. He develops a true sense of humility and becomes less anxious about the war. He continues to battle sensual temptations, but he fully commits himself to abstinence prior to marriage and monogamy if he is to get married.

He soon falls in love with a dedicated Christian girl. Her charitable and loving family welcomes him into their home and introduces him to a new circle of friends who all share the same values and beliefs. He feels content in his new circumstances but also humble and grateful.

The war is moving closer to home, and his prayers intensify appealing directly to God for guidance. During an air raid he does not perform any spectacular act of heroism, but he sticks to his post and fulfills his duties even in the face of great danger and fear. He learns to manage his emotions and fatigue while still maintaining hope.

The climax comes at the end of the book when the man dies in a subsequent air raid. As he is ushered into Heaven, his eyes are opened to witness the spiritual warfare that has surrounded his life. In this state of grace, he fully realizes that his death was the apex of the battle for his soul, and now he can rest knowing that he is safe.

Lewis masterfully provides a great analogy between the external war and the spiritual war raging inside the man. Both require great endurance, perseverance, and bravery, and the man's response to it, as with all life circumstances, is what ultimately shaped who he was and whose he was.

This story can easily be our story. In everyday life situations, we can choose God's will or evil's will, but we always have a choice. From the Christian perspective, to be ignorant of the spiritual realm and demonic strategies to influence choices and exploit our weakness is dangerous. Fortunately, as Christians we have been sealed with the Holy Spirit who provides us clarity of thought and cuts through devilish manipulations so that we might discover refreshing, simple, and straightforward truth.

CHARACTER SUMMARY

SCREWTAPE

Screwtape is a very formidable demon and an undersecretary in the lowerarchy of Hell. He is subtle, smart, arrogant, clever, hate-filled, and vicious with no love or regard for human beings. His job is to provide guidance and direction to young tempters out in the field. He is an experienced, older demon who understands a great deal about human nature and would love nothing more than to corrupt and damn man to an eternity of Hell.

Each letter is written by Screwtape and addressed to his nephew, Wormwood. The narrative is told in his voice. At times he appears affable to Wormwood, but he can also be very condescending with little patience for this young demon and easily frustrated by his irresponsibility. He quickly lets him know who the more superior demon is when Wormwood tries to betray him.

Screwtape refers to God as the "Enemy" and Satan as "Our Father Below." He is a bureaucrat well versed in history as well as rules and regulations. He knows how to manipulate the inner workings of the departments of Hell to obtain what he needs, and he is an ardent patriot to his cause and a connoisseur of those demons who are not.

WORMWOOD

Wormwood is Screwtape's incompetent nephew serving under his tutelage. This young demon's job, to whom all the letters are written, is to condemn the patient he has been assigned to Hell.

Wormwood is irresponsible, lazy, and immature. Being portrayed as one full of youthful ignorance, Wormwood would rather put his efforts into less effective methods while allowing Uncle Screwtape to do all the heavy lifting. Even though he is constantly chided by Screwtape for his numerous blunders, he remains optimistic that everything will be all right.

He would love nothing more than to reveal himself to his patient and to spend his time enjoying the human suffering brought about by war. Screwtape believes the irresponsible Wormwood is shirking his duties of performing the necessary research about his subject and human nature for more fanciful but less damaging methods of condemning the patient.

In the end, his failure is evident, and Wormwood appeals to his Uncle Screwtape for mercy of which there is none.

THE PATIENT

The patient is an ordinary young man living in England during the tumultuous years of World War II. His contemplation of Christianity and subsequent daily actions and thoughts are the subject of the letters between Screwtape and Wormwood.

He is thoughtful, honest, intellectual, sincere and fully aware of his weaknesses. His newfound faith and the realization of the power negative influences have on his life bring about an examination of those friends whom he enjoys spending time with. He also learns that simple, ordinary pleasures are enough to sustain him when he finds his faith drifting.

The patient finds moral strength within him as he battles a series of sexual temptations that lessen with each resistance. His courage is also put to the test as he bravely and honorably serves his country during the war. As a soldier, he eventually gives his life and is immediately ushered into presence of God.

THE PATIENT'S FIANCE

The patient's fiancé is a kind, loving, attractive, and dedicated young Christian woman. She is a virgin, full of virtues, and portrayed as an extraordinarily good person—just the sort of human that Screwtape loathes. He sees her as vile, sneaking, mouse-like, watery, and insignificant. She is just the type that Screwtape would have loved to see fed to the lions in the early days.

The girl comes from a charitable and loving Christian family who welcomes the patient into their home. They also introduce him to a new circle of friends who all share the same values and beliefs. Her one weakness that Screwtape desires to exploit is a narrowly defined understanding of her faith, but this is mostly due to ignorance and not spiritual pride.

THE PATIENT'S MOTHER

The patient lives with his mother who is a Christian. Having taught her son Christianity as a boy, it appears there might have been some friction between the two after his passionate conversion as a young man. The mother battles a form of gluttony that keeps her occupied with a strict diet and inevitably creates division between her family and friends.

THE ENEMY (God)

God is characterized as an ever-present, powerful being capable of loving "human vermin"—something Screwtape cannot understand. God is portrayed as participating in a spiritual battle with the Devil for the souls of men. God is distinguished by actually caring for and responding to their thoughts, needs, and concerns. However, God has left humans with the ability to choose which is where Screwtape and other demons get their foothold.

OUR FATHER BELOW (The Devil)

The Devil, worshiped by Screwtape and other demons, is unable to understand God's love for his creation. He claims to have left Heaven on his own accord and that all other stories are just rumors. He desires to damn as many souls to Hell as possible by corrupting human nature. There is no love in his dominion of Hell, even among fellow demons, but rather a competitive nature of eat or be eaten.

SLUBGOB (The Head of the Training College)

Slubgob is the principal of the Training College for Young Tempters. Screwtape portrays him initially as inept—churning out incompetent young demons, but later he treats him very graciously at an annual dinner.

GLUBOSE (The demon in charge of the patient's mother)

Glubose, possibly a combination of "Gluttony" and "Obese", is the demon in charge of the patient's mother. Although rarely mentioned, his job is to busy himself causing discord between her and her son as well as making her constant dietary restrictions a problem with her family and friends.

SLUMTRIMPET (The demon in charge of the patient's fiancé)

Slumtrimpet is a young female devil in charge of the patient's fiancé. She has very little success tempting the young woman into any kind of serious sin.

Course Notes and Study Format

HOW TO USE THIS GUIDE

In most editions, *The Screwtape Letters* consists of thirty-one letters and the additional *Screwtape Proposes a Toast*. This study guide does not include discussion questions for the toast, but you will find that available on line at www.ScrewtapeLettersStudyGuide.com. This study guide can be used for individual study or as a group study meeting weekly to discuss each letter.

STUDYING

Each week you will read three letters, which are approximately 5 pages each. Each letter is short but not easily digested, so allow time to ponder each letter thoroughly. As you read, make notes in your book and underline or highlight sections that interest you. You will find it helpful to number each paragraph within each letter as the study questions make reference to them. As you work through each session, make note of any other questions you have in the Notes section at the end of each study. The answers to each question can be found at www.ScrewtapeLettersStudyGuide.com. However, do not cheat yourself. Work through each session prior to viewing the answers.

GROUP FORMAT

For group formats, the study works well over 12 consecutive weeks. The first week is an introduction week to hand out study guides (if purchased by the church), read through the introduction and character sketches, and set a plan and schedule for the remaining 11 weeks. You might also have those who have previously read the book share their thoughts and experiences with it.

This study can certainly be used by Sunday school classes, but recognize that Sunday morning time in many churches is relatively short. Thus, the study lends itself very well to midweek times at the church or in the homes of members. Session length is variable. Ideally, you should allow at least 90 minutes per session. For longer sessions, take a quick refreshment break in the middle.

As a group leader, your role will be to facilitate the group sessions using the study guide and the answers found at www.ScrewtapeLettersStudyGuide.com. Recognize that you are the facilitator.

You are not the answer person; you are not the authority; you are not the judge to decide if responses are right or wrong. You are simply the person who tries to keep the discussion on track and in the time frame allowed while keeping everyone involved, heard, and respected.

LEARNING ENVIRONMENT

The following are some suggestions for shaping the learning environment for group sessions that help manage time, participation, and confidentiality.

- Ask the Holy Spirit for help as you prepare for the study. Pray for discernment for each member of the group, including yourself.
- Before each session, familiarize yourself with the questions and answers as it may have been several days since you completed the session. Consider reading the weekly letters again.
- Be prepared to adjust the session as group members interact and questions arise. Allow for the Holy Spirit to move in and through the material, the group members, and yourself.
- Arrange the meeting space to enhance the learning process. Group members should be seated around a table or in a circle so that they can all see one another. Moveable chairs are best.
- Download the quick Bible reference handout which includes all the verses for each study available at www.ScrewtapeLettersStudyGuide.com and distribute at the beginning of class to save time.
- Bring Bibles for those who forget to bring one or for those who might not have one. (If someone is reading aloud, you might ask the person to identify from which Bible translation he or she is reading.)
- If your teaching style includes recording responses from participants or writing questions or quotations for discussion on a board you may want access to a whiteboard or an easel.
- Agree on the class schedule and times. In order to maintain continuity, it would be best if your class meets for twelve consecutive weeks.
- The suggested session time is 90 minutes. Because each letter can lead to substantial discussion, you may need to make choices about what you will cover, or you may choose to extend your group sessions to allow more time for discussion.
- Create a climate where it is safe to share. Encourage group members to participate as they feel comfortable. Remember that some will be eager to give answers or offer commentary while others will need time to process and think.
- If you notice that some participants are hesitant to enter the conversation, ask if they have thoughts to share. Give everyone an opportunity to talk, but keep the conversation moving. Intervene when necessary to prevent a few individuals from dominating discussion.

- If no one answers at first during a discussion, do not be afraid of silence. Count silently to ten, and then say, "Would anyone like to go first?" If no one responds, provide your own answer and ask for reactions. If you limit your sharing to a surface level, others will follow suit. Keep in mind that if your group is new, cohesion might take a couple of weeks to form. If group members do not share at first, give them time.
- Encourage multiple answers or responses before moving on.
- Ask, "Why?" or "Why do you believe that?" or "Can you say more about that?" to draw out greater depth from a response.
- Affirm others' responses with comments such as "Great" or "Thanks" or "Good insight"—especially if this is the first time someone has spoken during the group session.
- Monitor your own contributions. If you are doing most of the talking, back off so that you do not train the group to listen rather than speak.
- Honor the designated time window. Begin on time. If a session runs longer than expected, get consensus from the group before continuing.
- Involve participants in various aspects of the session such as offering prayer and reading Scripture.
- Because some questions call for sharing personal experiences, confidentiality is essential. Remind group members at each session of the importance of confidentiality and of not passing along stories that have been shared in the group.

LETTER 1
REASON AND REALITY

Summary

In this letter, we learn that Wormwood has been making sure that his patient spends plenty of time with his materialistic friends. Wormwood believes that by using reason and argument he can keep the man from belief in God. Screwtape does not disagree that it is good to influence the man's thoughts, but he reminds Wormwood that his main job is to keep the patient from thinking too deeply about any spiritual matter. Instead he should use ordinary everyday distraction to mislead the man.

> *The trouble about argument is that it moves the whole struggle*
> *onto the Enemy's own ground.* - Screwtape

Discussion Questions

1. In what way does Screwtape say that Wormwood is being naive? ¶ 1

2. What is Screwtape's explanation of why Wormwood should avoid reliance on "argument"? ¶ 2

3. What is the connection between "thinking and doing", and how does this impact our daily lives? ¶ 1

4. Screwtape claims that people "having a dozen incompatible philosophies dancing together inside their head". What specifically does he credit for this? What do you think the other "weapons" are today? How can they be used to destroy argument? ¶ 1

5. If, according to Screwtape, people are not persuaded by what is true or false, what does he say people are concerned with? Why do people believe what they believe? ¶ 1

6. Read Hebrews 2:14-18. What is the "abominable advantage" God has over Satan? How should this encourage us in our Christian walk? ¶ 3

7. The story of the atheist in the British museum provides a dark and somewhat disturbing insight into rather pleasant distractions that can draw us away from spiritual matters. In this particular instance, the atheist's appetite was enough to pull him away from his train of thought in which God was working. How can Satan use common distractions to create detours in the course of our daily lives? ¶ 3

8. Why would Screwtape advise Wormwood to "Keep pressing home on him the *ordinariness* of things."? What "comfort zones" in our Christian walk do we need to be cautious of? ¶ 4

9. Read Luke 10:39-42. What ordinary everyday distractions was Martha concerned with? Who did it make her resent? What did she miss out on?

Answer Guide Available at www.ScrewtapeLettersStudyGuide.com

Discussion Notes:

LETTER 2
DISTRACTING THE CHRISTIAN MIND

Screwtape begins this letter by rebuking Wormwood for letting his patient escape him and become a Christian. However, all is not lost. If he can cause the man to become disillusioned with the church by highlighting the strange habits and hypocrisies of its members, Wormwood still might succeed. Screwtape tells Wormwood to attack the man's spiritual immaturity in an effort to win him back.

> *The Enemy allows this disappointment to occur*
> *on the threshold of every human endeavour.* – Screwtape

Discussion Questions

1. "There's no need to despair," Screwtape writes. "Hundreds of these adult converts have been reclaimed after a brief sojourn in the Enemy's camp and are now with us." What is Lewis alluding to in this passage? ¶ 1

2. Why does Screwtape suggest, "All the habits of the patient, both mental and bodily, are still in our favor"? ¶ 1

3. Screwtape claims, "One of our great allies at present is the Church itself." What strategies might tempters employ with new Christians to create dissatisfaction with the church? ¶ 2

4. Consider yourself a new Christian who has just walked into your church for the first time. What expectations might you have about fellow church members, the leadership, the church, and the worship service?

5. Screwtape tells Wormwood to keep the patient focused on the visible church. St. Augustine wrote there is a "visible" and "invisible" church in Christianity. How would you describe these two churches, and why does Screwtape believe it is important to keep the patient fixed to the "visible"?

6. Screwtape claims the patient "has an idea of 'Christians' in his mind, which he supposes to be spiritual but which is, in fact, largely pictorial." What romanticized view of Christianity might a new convert have of their spiritual life? ¶ 2

7. In regards to our disappointment, Screwtape said, "Work hard, then, on the disappointment or anticlimax which is certainly coming to the patient during his first few weeks as a churchman." For what purpose might God allow disappointment to occur on the threshold of every human endeavor? What is the result if we get through the "initial dryness"? ¶ 3

8. After all of this, Screwtape provides Wormwood the perfect means to attack his patient. "He [the patient] has not been anything like long enough with the Enemy to have any real humility yet." Why is humility for a new believer so important? What is the importance of humility in the Christian life? ¶ 4

Answer Guide Available at www.ScrewtapeLettersStudyGuide.com

Notes:

LETTER 3
RELATIONSHIPS

In this third letter, Screwtape suggests that Wormwood focus on the patient's relationship with his mother. By cooperating with Glubose, the demon who is working on the mother, Screwtape imparts secrets on how to slowly deteriorate the relationship.

> *You must bring him to a condition in which he can practise self-examination for an hour without discovering any of those facts about himself which are perfectly clear to anyone who has ever lived in the same house with him or worked in the same office.* - Screwtape

Discussion Questions

1. Read Romans 12: 2 and 1 Timothy 4:16. How is God working "from the center outward" to transform our conduct to his standard?

2. What is the first method of temptation that Screwtape suggests using on the patient? ¶ 2

3. Read John 14:15, 1 John 5:3 and Ephesians 6:6. Screwtape says the patient thinks "his conversion is something inside him." What is conversion if it's more than just a commitment to a heart change? ¶ 2

4. Although seemingly counter intuitive, why would Screwtape want Wormwood to have the "patient" practice an hour of self-examination "without discovering any of those facts about himself which are perfectly clear to anyone who has ever lived in the same house with him or worked in the same office"? ¶ 2

5. What is the second method of temptation that Screwtape suggests using on the patient? ¶ 3

6. What methods does Screwtape suggest Wormwood employ to render the patient's prayers for his mother innocuous? ¶ 3

7. What are the two advantages that Screwtape says will occur by employing this method? ¶ 3

8. Read Luke 18:1. What motivates the Pharisee to pray? How should we approach God when praying for others?

9. What is the third method of temptation that Screwtape suggests using on the patient? ¶ 4

10. What annoying habits of others irritate you? Which of your annoying habits do you think irritate others?

11. What is the fourth method of temptation that Screwtape suggests using on the patient? ¶ 5

12. What is the "double standard" Screwtape encourages between the patient and his mother? ¶ 5

13. Provide an example of something being said "with the express purpose of offending and yet having a grievance when offence is taken".

14. At the end of the letter, Screwtape wants Wormwood to search out whether the mother is jealous of her son's recent conversion. How is this similar to the story of the 'elder brother' in the parable of the Prodigal Son in Luke 15:11-32? ¶ 6

Answer Guide Available at www.ScrewtapeLettersStudyGuide.com

Notes:

LETTER 4
SINCERE PRAYER

Screwtape is insulted by Wormwood's last letter to him on the topic of prayer in which Wormwood attempts to assign blame for his mistakes on Screwtape. As a result, Screwtape provides a more in depth discussion on the subject of prayer telling Wormwood that he should keep his patient from seriously intending to pray at all. If that fails, Wormwood should misdirect the focus of the patient's prayers so they are only about himself or an object rather than another person.

> *It is funny how mortals always picture us as putting things into their minds: in reality our best work is done by keeping things out.* – Screwtape

Discussion Questions

1. Screwtape encourages Wormwood to keep his patient from praying altogether. How does this contrast to God's direction in the following verses: Luke 18:1; Colossians 4:2; 1 Thessalonians 5:16-18? ¶ 2

2. What is Lewis referring to in the comment about the "parrot-like nature" of prayers? ¶ 2

3. Read Matthew 6:5-9. How does Jesus respond to this same question?

4. What is the difference between producing in ourselves "a vaguely devotional *mood* in which real concentration of will and intelligence have no part" as opposed to what Screwtape refers to as a "prayer of silence" that is used by those very advanced in the Enemy's service? ¶ 2

5. Read John 4:24. What sort of balance must take place between our emotions (or spontaneous prayer) and more formal prayers like what we find in the Disciple's Prayer in Matthew 6:9-15?

6. How does 1 John 1:9 relate to praying for forgiveness and our desire to feel forgiven?

7. What does Screwtape mean when he writes that humans don't "start from a direct perception of Him"? ¶ 4

8. Screwtape likes imaginary pictures of God as a focus for prayer. What mental images of God do we create in our mind?

9. Why does Screwtape say that we do not desire the "real nakedness of the soul" as much as we suppose? ¶ 4

10. What does God say in Ecclesiastes 5:4 about making bold claims in our prayer life?

Answer Guide Available at www.ScrewtapeLettersStudyGuide.com

Notes:

LETTER 5
WAR

Screwtape begins this letter by once again reprimanding Wormwood for his naivety and his excitement about a "new war" in Europe. Screwtape explains that war can be very entertaining in so much as it brings about hatred and violence, but it can also drive masses of people to God. Screwtape warns his nephew not to get caught up in the enjoyment only to lose his patient to God.

> *When I see the temporal suffering of humans who finally escape us, I feel as if I had been allowed to taste the first course of a rich banquet and then denied the rest. It is worse than not to have tasted it at all.* – Screwtape

Discussion Questions

1. Screwtape warns Wormwood not to be overly confident in "terror-pictures of the future" and "self pitying glances" of the past that Wormwood has used to scare the "patient." Read Luke 9: 61-62. How does Jesus use the plow to illustrate our attention to our past and future? ¶ 1

2. What is Screwtape's attitude toward war? Does it surprise you? ¶ 1

3. What is the "real business" that Wormwood is to be about? Provide examples of how our faith is diabolically assaulted and the development of virtues are hindered? ¶ 1

4. Why does Screwtape say it does not make any difference whether Wormwood's patient is "an extreme patriot or an ardent pacifist?" ¶ 1

5. What is the "blockade" that God is imposing on Screwtape and other demons? ¶ 2

6. Read Romans 5:3-5; 1 Peter 5:10; and James 1:2-4. How does God use suffering in the life of a Christian?

7. U. S. Military Chaplain William Thomas Cummings in a field sermon during the Battle of Bataan in 1942 is quoted as saying, "There are no atheists in foxholes." What does this saying mean? Would Screwtape agree or disagree and why? ¶ 2

8. From Screwtape's perspective, why is it better if humans died in a nursing home rather than a war? ¶ 2

9. What does Screwtape mean by "a faith which is destroyed by a war or a pestilence cannot really have been worth the trouble of destroying"? ¶ 3

Notes:

LETTER 6
FOCUS

Military service seems inevitable for Wormwood's patient, and Screwtape affirms the decision to cultivate anxiety and fear about the future. Wormwood's first goal for the patient is to divert his attention away from God and the good he should be doing. Secondly, Wormwood should seek to transfer the patient's hatred for the war on to his everyday neighbors.

> *He wants men to be concerned with what they do; our business is to*
> *keep them thinking about what will happen to them.* - Screwtape

Discussion Questions

1. Read Mark 4:18-19. How can suspense and anxiety "barricade" a person's mind against God? How does Satan benefit by keeping us anxious about things that may never happen? According to Philippians 4:6, what should be our approach to anxiety? ¶ 1

2. What does Screwtape mean when he writes, "It is your business to see that the patient never thinks of the present fear as his appointed cross, but only of the things he is afraid of?" Read Luke 9:23. What does it mean to pick up your cross daily and follow Christ? What insight can we gain from this about the nature of anxiety and the way it misleads us? ¶ 2

3. "We have nothing to fear, but fear itself." This famous line used in the first inaugural address of Franklin D. Roosevelt was given during the depths of the depression in 1933. Why does Screwtape encourage Wormwood to divert the patient's mind "from the thing feared to fear itself?" ¶ 3

4. What is this "general rule" Screwtape is referring to? How can Satan use this strategy in our prayer life? ¶ 3

5. Why does Screwtape write that getting people to hate distant enemies is disappointing? Why is it easier to hate those who are close and to be charitable toward those who are far away? ¶ 4

6. How does Screwtape suggest getting the patient to the point where his malice is real and his benevolence is imaginary? ¶ 5

7. Draw and then explain below the concentric circles that Screwtape says are the three levels to a human being. At what point in the circle does Lewis say that a person is authentically living the Christian life? ¶ 5

8. What does Screwtape mean when he insists that Wormwood "must keep on shoving all the virtues outward till they are finally located in the circle of fantasy, and all the desirable qualities inward toward the Will"? ¶ 5

Answer Guide Available at www.ScrewtapeLettersStudyGuide.com

Notes:

LETTER 7
EXTREMISM

Wormwood (due to youth and inexperience) has asked Screwtape if he should reveal himself to the patient. In this letter, Screwtape tells him that the current policy is to keep humans ignorant of their existence. Screwtape also follows up on a previous discussion of whether Wormwood should try to influence the man to become a fervent patriot or an extreme pacifist during the war. Screwtape advises that in the end it really does not matter as long as he misdirects the patient's thoughts away from God and others.

> *Once you have made the World an end, and faith a means, you have almost won your man, and it makes very little difference what kind of worldly end he is pursuing. –* Screwtape

Discussion Questions

1. According to Screwtape, what is the "cruel dilemma" demons face in deciding whether or not to making their existence known to man? ¶ 1

2. Do comic figures or benign illustrations of 'devils' assist in the work of Screwtape and Wormwood? How does the media inhibit our belief in demons and spirits? ¶ 1

3. At the time this letter was written (Remember the setting is during World War II.), Screwtape claims it is their policy to conceal themselves. What about today? Would you say that at the present time Screwtape would still say to keep demonic existence a secret? ¶ 1

4. What does Screwtape claim is a devil's "perfect work"? ¶ 1

5. How does Screwtape explain to Wormwood the scheme behind deciding whether to lull people to complacency or to inflame them into extremism? ¶ 2

6. Screwtape suggests that the church, although heavily guarded, has proven successful in exploiting extremism by creating subordinate factions. What extremism do we find in the church today? From a Christian perspective, is there any extremism to be desired? ¶ 2

7. If you were to take a poll of the Christians you know, would patriotism or pacifism be considered the more godly position and why?

8. What is Screwtape's advice to Wormwood regarding how he should decide whether to push extreme patriotism or pacifism? ¶ 3

9. Screwtape encourages Wormwood to take the patient's passion (the "Cause") and make it part of his faith so that it appears as though he is sacrificing for the "Cause." As Christians, what can we learn from this? ¶ 4

10. What does Ecclesiastes 7:18-20 say about avoiding extremes?

Answer Guide Available at www.ScrewtapeLettersStudyGuide.com

Notes:

LETTER 8
TROUGHS AND PEAKS

In the eighth letter, it is obvious that Screwtape is becoming increasingly annoyed with Wormwood's inexperience and naïve enthusiasm. Wormwood's hopes that his Patient's religious phase is dying away are quickly dashed by Screwtape's explanation of the law of Undulation, details of God's master plan for humans, and how those plans contrast to Satan's master plans.

> *Our cause is never more in danger than when a human, no longer desiring, but still intending, to do our Enemy's will, looks round upon a universe from which every trace of Him seems to have vanished, and asks why he has been forsaken, and still obeys.* – Screwtape

Discussion Questions

1. How does Screwtape explain the law of Undulation? How do you tend to respond to the ups and downs of your spiritual journey? ¶ 2

2. Explain Screwtape's assessment of human nature as "amphibians"—half spirit and half animals. ¶ 2

3. Read James 1:2-4 and Romans 5:3. Why does God rely on the "troughs" or trials even more than on the "peaks" in our lives? ¶ 3

4. Fill in the blanks. Humans are primarily _____ to Screwtape and his workers for the purpose of _____ the human's will into theirs. ¶ 3

5. Explain how Ephesians 4:22-24 supports Screwtape's argument that God wants to fill the universe with little replicas of Himself who voluntarily choose to love and serve Him? ¶ 3

6. Screwtape provides a direct comparison between the relationship that God wants to have with us and the relationship that Satan desires. ¶ 3

God's relationship with us	Satan's relationship with us
1. *Servants to become sons*	*Cattle to become food*
2.	
3.	
4.	

7. The definition of ravish is to "seize and carry off (someone) by force". The definition of woo is to "try to gain the love of someone." So then, what does Screwtape mean by saying God "cannot ravish. He can only woo"? ¶ 4

8. What does Screwtape mean by, "He cannot 'tempt' to virtue as we do to 'vice'"? ¶ 4

9. Screwtape said that their cause is never more in danger than when someone "no longer desiring, but still intending, to do [God's] will, looks round upon a universe from which every trace of Him seems to have vanished, and asks why he has been forsaken, and still obeys." If we possess this attitude, what statement does this make about our view of God?

Answer Guide Available at www.ScrewtapeLettersStudyGuide.com

Notes:

LETTER 9
PLEASURES

In this letter, Screwtape advises Wormwood on how best to exploit his patient's spiritual dry period by first trapping the man with sensual pleasures (especially sex) then by attacking his faith directly. Screwtape also discusses the subject of pleasure in its original, pure form as designed by God, and he explains how Satan perverts pleasure and transforms it into sin.

> *Never forget that when we are dealing with any pleasure in its healthy and normal and satisfying form, we are, in a sense, on the Enemy's ground. I know we have won many a soul through pleasure.* – Screwtape

Discussion Questions

1. Why did Screwtape say that one of the most effective methods of tempting people during the "trough periods" is through sexual temptation? Why is it not as effective during our peak periods? ¶ 2

2. What does Screwtape mean by, "Never forget that when we are dealing with any pleasure in its healthy and normal and satisfying form, we are, in a sense, on the Enemy's ground?" What is the workaround Screwtape suggests to Wormwood? ¶ 2

3. What does Screwtape suggest about temptation when he says, "An ever increasing craving for an ever diminishing pleasure is the formula"? What is God's solution as found in 1 Corinthians 10:13-14? ¶ 2

4. What is another way Screwtape suggests exploiting the dry spell that the patient is going through? ¶ 3

5. How would these thoughts affect us as either a pessimist or an optimist? ¶ 3

6. Screwtape said, "A moderated religion is as good for us as no religion at all." How does Revelations 3:15-16 support this statement? ¶ 3

7. What is another option that Screwtape mentions as a means to exploit the patient during his dry spell? ¶ 4

8. How does introducing "phases" into our thoughts work to Satan's advantage? ¶ 4

Notes:

LETTER 10
BAD FRIENDS

In this letter, Screwtape approves of Wormwood's efforts to encourage a spiritually harmful relationship that his patient has developed with a couple that is fun, bright, wealthy, and worldly. This relationship will prove to be more effective if he can guide the man into leading a double life, one at church and another with his new friends.

> *All mortals tend to turn into the thing they are pretending to be.* – Screwtape

Discussion Questions

1. How does Screwtape describe the middle-aged married couple that has just come into the patient's life? ¶ 1

2. How could all of these social sets become a snare for a Christian and especially for a new convert? What social sets are snares for you? ¶ 1

3. What is the danger or trap that we can fall into when we find ourselves in relationships with friends whose faith doesn't coincide with our own? ¶ 2

4. What does Screwtape mean by saying "All mortals tend to turn into the thing they are pretending to be"? ¶ 2

5. If the statement above is true, what does 3 John 1:11; 1 Corinthians 11:1; and Philippians 2:5 say about how we guard ourselves against compromising on our faith?

6. Screwtape says that he sees a lot of modern Christian writings about Mammon (the worship of material wealth and greed) but little about worldly vanities, choice of friends, and the value of time. What does Screwtape give as the reason for that? ¶ 3

7. What does 1 John 2:15-17 say about how Christians are to be separate from the world?

8. There are three tactics Screwtape advises Wormwood to employ once the patient realizes that his faith and friends do not match up. Which tactic to use will depend on his patient's level of stupidity. Describe them below: ¶ 4

      a. Parallel Lives

      b. Exploit his Vanity

      c. Doing sinners good by hanging around them

Notes:

LETTER 11
LAUGHTER

Wormwood's patient has found a new set of sophisticated friends who are suitable to Screwtape because they are "consistent scoffers and worldlings" as well as "great laughers." Screwtape feels it is important, at this point, to explore the subject of laughter and to explain why it is not always in the devil's favor.

> *Only a clever human can make a real Joke about virtue, or indeed about anything else; any of them can be trained to talk as if virtue were funny.* – Screwtape

Discussion Questions

1. How can someone "progress quietly and comfortably" towards Hell without ever committing any "spectacular crimes?" ¶ 1

2. In English, the word "scoffer" can mean "one who mocks, ridicules, or scorns the belief of another." In Hebrew, the word translated "scoffer" or "mocker" can also mean "ambassador." So a scoffer is one who not only disagrees with an idea, but he also considers himself an ambassador for the opposing idea. Read Proverbs 29:8 and Psalm 1:1. Ultimately, what is the scoffer's goal, and what is the Bible's counsel about joining in with scoffers?

3. What are the four causes of laughter and describe each of them below? ¶ 2

¶ 2	
¶ 3	
¶ 4	
¶ 6	

4. Screwtape says that he does not know the real cause of Joy. Read Romans 15:13 and Psalms 28:7. What does the Bible say is the source of joy?

5. Why is Screwtape not a fan of fun either? What is the only benefit of fun for Screwtape? ¶ 3

6. How can humor be an "invaluable means of destroying shame"? ¶ 5

7. Flippancy is defined as a "lack of respect or seriousness; frivolousness" especially when it comes to "grave or serious matters." How does a "habit of flippancy build up around someone an armor-plating against God"? ¶ 6

8. Read Psalm 19:14. How might this verse change the way we approach conversations, television, music, and the movies we consume?

Answer Guide Available at www.ScrewtapeLettersStudyGuide.com

Notes:

LETTER 12
NOTHING

Wormwood is having success helping his patient drift away from God. However, Screwtape fears that Wormwood might be moving too quickly and provides advice on how to carefully guide the patient on a slow path to Hell. Screwtape notes that the danger in rushing the process is that the man will awaken spiritually, realize where he is, and start making positive changes in his life.

> *Indeed the safest road to Hell is the gradual one—the gentle slope, soft underfoot, without sudden turnings, without milestones, without signposts.* – Screwtape

Discussion Questions

1. Why is it Satan's advantage to get us to believe that all of our choices are "trivial and revocable"? ¶ 1

2. How can the mere habit of church attendance be a snare to our spiritual life? ¶ 2

3. Screwtape said that having a "vague, uneasy feeling that we are not doing well" is better than recognizing clearly that we are being sinful. Why does Screwtape say this "dim uneasiness needs careful handling"? ¶ 2 & 3

4. Why does Screwtape suggest that when we are in the state of sin, we will dislike religious duties and hope they will be done quickly? ¶ 3

5. As the patient continues on this downward spiral, Screwtape says that "the uneasiness and his reluctance to face it" will "cut him off more and more from all real happiness". Do you think the patient's avoidance of Christians and Christian activities could be a synonymous with depression? Why or Why not? ¶ 4

6. Screwtape says, "It does not matter how small the sins are, provided that their cumulative effect is to edge the man away from the Light and out into the Nothing." Why doesn't it matter how small the sins are? ¶ 5

7. Compare Matthew 7: 13-14 with the "safest road to hell" that Screwtape describes? ¶ 5

Answer Guide Available at www.ScrewtapeLettersStudyGuide.com

Notes:

LETTER 13
PERSONAL PLEASURE

In this letter, Screwtape is not pleased with Wormwood. He has allowed his patient awaken from his spiritual drift and into reality by experiencing real, simple pleasures. Screwtape understands that this repentance and renewal can have a more profound effect on the patient than his original conversion. However, all is not lost says Screwtape, as long as Wormwood can keep the patient from acting on his new feelings.

> *The more often he feels without acting, the less he will be able ever to act, and, in the long run, the less he will be able to feel.* – Screwtape

Discussion Questions

1. Screwtape refers to the man's spiritual change as a "second conversion". In some circles this might be referred to as a "rededication of one's life." How would you describe this phase and have you had a similar experience? ¶ 1

2. What is the "asphyxiating cloud" that Screwtape is referring to? Read 2 Timothy 1:14 and 1 John 5:18. How do these verses support Wormwood's inability to attack his patient? How do we get to that point where we are surrounded by God's "asphyxiating cloud"? ¶ 2

3. What does Screwtape say about the dangers of "real" Pain and Pleasure? ¶ 3

4. Screwtape says that Wormwood has failed to employ either Romantic or Worldly methods of temptation. Describe each of these methods. ¶ 3

5. In Romans 12:2, what instruction does Paul provide for protecting ourselves against a culture that is trying to sell us "vanity, bustle, irony, and expensive tedium as pleasures"?

6. What is the difference in the ways in which God and Satan want to detach people from themselves? ¶ 4

7. Why would Screwtape want to eradicate simple pleasures like "enjoying country crickets or collecting stamps or drinking cocoa" from our life? What are some examples of innocent pleasures that if you stopped enjoying, might weaken your will? ¶ 4

8. Now that Wormwood's patient has experienced these simple pleasures, what does Screwtape say is the thing to do next? ¶ 5

9. What does Screwtape mean by "The more often he feels without acting, the less he will be able to act, and, in the long run, the less he will be able to feel?" ¶ 5

Answer Guide Available at www.ScrewtapeLettersStudyGuide.com

Notes:

LETTER 14
HUMILITY

In this letter, Screwtape is concerned because Wormwood's patient has discovered real humility. Screwtape tells Wormwood to draw the patient's attention to himself and to just how humble he is being. As the patient becomes proud of his newfound humility and false modesty, the actual virtue of humility becomes worthless and he becomes susceptible to temptation.

> *The Enemy wants to bring the man to a state of mind in which he could design the best cathedral in the world, and know it to be the best, and rejoice in the fact, without being any more (or less) or otherwise glad at having done it than he would be if it had been done by another.* – Screwtape

Discussion Questions

1. Screwtape says that he likes it when people make "confident resolutions" at their conversion experience. What confident resolutions might we make when we first accept Christ? How might this change as we mature as Christians? ¶ 1

2. What does Screwtape mean by, "All virtues are less formidable to us once the man is aware that he has them…"? What is the danger in making the man aware of his virtue? ¶ 2

3. Why does Screwtape instruct Wormwood to confuse humility with low opinion? ¶ 4

4. Why is bad for a woman who really is pretty or a man who really is intelligent to believe they are not? ¶ 4

5. How does Romans 12:15 support the idea ". . . that he [the patient] can rejoice in his own talents as frankly and gratefully as in his neighbor's talents"? ¶ 4

6. How hard would it be for you to rejoice in your neighbor's talents and accomplishments in the following situations: ¶ 4
- Your neighbor's son scored the winning basket in the game while your son sat the bench.
- Your coworker achieved his sales goal and won a trip to Hawaii; you got a gift card to Starbucks.
- Your sister is pregnant with their third child; you have not been able to conceive.
- Your best friend just got a great new job; you are unemployed.
- Everyone gushed over your sister's dessert at Thanksgiving; no one touched yours.

7. According to Ephesians 4:2, what is the type of humility that God wants from us? From Mark 12: 30-31, where does humility begin? ¶ 4

8. How does God counteract Satan's strategy of trying to instill vainglory or false modesty into the patient? ¶ 5

Answer Guide Available at www.ScrewtapeLettersStudyGuide.com

Notes:

LETTER 15
PAST, PRESENT, FUTURE, AND ETERNITY

Currently, the patient's anxiety level is low due to a lull in the war. Screwtape instructs Wormwood to direct the patient's attention to either the past (which is gone) or to the future (which does not exist) but never to his present state. Either strategy will work, but focusing on the future works best.

> *But we want a man hag-ridden by the Future—haunted by visions of an imminent heaven or hell upon earth—ready to break the Enemy's commands in the present if by so doing we make him think he can attain the one or avert the other—dependent for his faith on the success or failure of schemes whose end he will not live to see.* – Screwtape

Discussion Questions

1. What fears of the future distract you the most in your daily life? What is your line of defense when Satan starts attacking you with those fears?

2. According to Screwtape, what are the two things that God wants us to attend to and why? ¶ 2

3. Screwtape says, "For the present is the point at which time touches eternity." Why is living in the present—in contrast to past experiences or future expectations—most like eternity? ¶ 2

4. Why does Screwtape say that it is far better to make humans live in the future than in the past? ¶ 3

5. What do Jesus' words in Matthew 6:25-34 tell us about our preoccupation with the future?

6. God wants man to think about the Future too, "just so much as is necessary for *now* planning the acts of justice or charity which will probably be their duty tomorrow." What does Satan want man to think about the Future? ¶ 4

7. There are two ways that we can live in the moment—a right way and a wrong way. Describe those below: ¶ 5

The Right Way (or God's Way)	
The Wrong Way (or Satan's Way)	

8. Read Luke 12:16-21. What is Jesus' advice for those who are living in the moment but in the wrong way?

Answer Guide Available at www.ScrewtapeLettersStudyGuide.com

Notes:

LETTER 16
CHURCHES

In this letter, Screwtape questions why Wormwood has not encouraged his patient to church hop. Unless the patient is indifferent, Wormwood should help him become critical and dissatisfied with his church. Screwtape has identified two churches it the area that are full of factions and hatred, and both would be perfect for helping to damage the patient's faith.

> *Surely you know that if a man can't be cured of churchgoing, the next best thing is to send him all over the neighbourhood looking for the church that "suits" him until he becomes a taster or connoisseur of churches.* – Screwtape

Discussion Questions

1. Screwtape suggests sending the patient all over the neighborhood becoming a "taster or connoisseur of churches". "Church hoping" is as alive today as when Lewis wrote this book. Do you think churches today cater to the consumer mentality of the church hopper and if so, how do churches cater to it? ¶ 1

2. What is it about church hopping that can be destructive to a person's faith? What does 2 Timothy 4:3-5 say about the importance of finding a biblically-based church?

3. Identify and describe the two reasons why Screwtape says it is important to encourage the patient to church hop. ¶ 2

4. If you were looking for a church, what aspects of church would tempt you to be a critic when God wants you to be a student?

5. At the first of the two churches that Screwtape advises Wormwood to introduce to the man, the Vicar serves up a blend of diluted Christianity so watered down that he (the Vicar) "shocks his parishioners with his own unbelief". Why would this be dangerous for the patient? ¶ 3

6. The second of the two churches is led by a man "who cannot bring himself to preach anything which is not calculated to shock, grieve, puzzle, or humiliate." Why would this be dangerous to the patient? ¶ 4

7. What is Screwtape's definition of a "party church"? ¶ 5

8. According to Screwtape, what is the "real fun" in creating factions between churches? How do you see this playing out in denominations today, and what is the real danger? ¶ 5

9. In an effort to avoid factions, what is Paul's counsel to us in Romans 14:19-21regarding "the human without scruples" always giving in "to the human with scruples"? ¶ 5

Answer Guide Available at www.ScrewtapeLettersStudyGuide.com

Notes:

LETTER 17
GLUTTONY

In this letter, Screwtape helps Wormwood understand that the sin of gluttony is just as alive today as it always was—but with a new modern twist. This mutated form of gluttony is not **necessarily about how much a person eats,** but rather about being controlled by what one eats. This control often manifests itself in the form of inconvenient demands on others.

> *If he must think of the medical side of chastity, feed him the grand lie which we have made the English humans believe, the physical exercise in excess and consequent fatigue are specially favorable to this virtue.* - Screwtape

Discussion Questions

1. Screwtape says that we seldom think of gluttony as sin anymore, and it is very rarely preached about. This is due in large part to the successful strategy of demons to focus efforts on the Gluttony of Delicacy and not on the Gluttony of Excess. What is the difference between the two? Toward which type of gluttony are you inclined? ¶ 1

    a.   Gluttony of Excess –

    b.   Gluttony of Delicacy –

2. What behaviors and characteristics of the patient's mother identify her as a good example of Gluttony of Delicacy? ¶ 1

3. Read 1 Corinthians 9: 24-27. The word "discipline" literally means "to beat black and blue." Using the analogy of an athlete, what is Paul telling us in this passage about how to maintain self-control and not becoming a slave to our bodies?

4. Screwtape's representation of the inner operation of demons is described as "quiet, unobtrusive work". Why is this disturbing? What is the danger in a demon rushing the process with the patient's mother? ¶ 2

5. What is the "All-I-want" state of mind that Screwtape describes about the patient's mother? How does this mentality shape her life and affect those around her? ¶ 2

6. How does Glubose counteract the Spirits promptings on the mother when He suggests that perhaps "she is too interested in food"? ¶ 2

7. Why do you think Screwtape believes males are more inclined to an expression of gluttony that reveals itself in the form of vanity? What does he hope the vanity turns into? ¶ 3

8. What do gluttony and sexual immorality have in common as far as self-control? How is it a deception that "physical exercise in excess and consequent fatigue are specially favorable to" the virtue of chastity? ¶ 4

Answer Guide Available at www.ScrewtapeLettersStudyGuide.com

Notes:

LETTER 18
LOVE AND MARRIAGE

In this letter, Screwtape helps Wormwood understand that God's standard regarding sexual activity is either abstinence or monogamy within marriage. Screwtape then explains the drastically different perspectives between God and Satan on the designs of sexual union between a man and a woman.

> *The whole philosophy of Hell rests on recognition of the axiom that one thing is not another thing, and, specially, that one self is not another self. My good is my good and your good is yours. What one gains another loses.* – Screwtape

Discussion Questions

1. According to Screwtape, what dilemma has God placed on the human race in regards to His demands on sexuality and why is this a dilemma? ¶ 2

2. Screwtape says he wants people to think that, "being in love is the only respectable grounds for marriage" and when those feelings fade, the marriage is "no longer binding." If a marriage should not be based on feelings of being in love, on what should it be based? ¶ 2

3. Hell finds very useful the idea of "falling in love". What problems do you think can arise when a couple gives in to the transient emotions or feelings of "being in love"?

4. If God also gave us feelings and emotions, how can these feelings of "being in love" be wrong? How does Paul define love in 1 Corinthians 13:4-7?

5. Read Ephesians 5:21-33. What does this passage tell us about the quality of love that husbands and wives are to have for each other?

6. Why does Screwtape compare the philosophy of Hell to that of a competition? ¶ 3

7. Screwtape says that God's philosophy contradicts that of Satan's. How? ¶ 4

8. In Ephesians 5:28-33, how does Paul define "one flesh"? What is the purpose of this transcendental and eternal state of being that happens when a couple unites as one flesh? ¶ 6

Notes:

LETTER 19
USING LOVE

Screwtape has become a little concerned by Wormwood's previous letter. In his previous letters, Screwtape blundered by uttering that the "Enemy really loves His creatures." This would be considered heresy in the devil's world, and Screwtape feels it best to explain it away through cynicism. However, he continues his talk on the subject of love noting that either the acceptance or rejection of "falling in love" can be useful if focused in the right way.

> *And there lies the great task. We know that He cannot really love: nobody can: it doesn't make sense. If we could only find out what He is <u>really</u> up to! Hypothesis after hypothesis has been tried, and still we can't find out.* – Screwtape

Discussion Questions

1. Screwtape displays his cynicism of God's love when he says, "He is one being, they are distinct from Him. Their good cannot be His. All His talk about Love must be a disguise for something else—He must have some *real* motive for creating them and taking so much trouble about them." Why is hard for some people to believe there is a God who is not motivated by anything other than pure love for His creation? ¶ 2

2. There are obviously those who, if given the opportunity, would choose to take advantage of others for personal gain. But, if we are not careful, having a constantly cynical attitude will harden our hearts, and eventually we will trust no one. How do you find a balance between healthy skepticism and hard-hearted cynicism?

3. Read Genesis 1:27 and John 3:16. According to these verses, why do you think God loves the world, and how did He show His love?

4. From Screwtape's perspective, what was the "chief cause of our Father's quarrel with the Enemy"? What does Isaiah 14:12-15 and Ezekiel 28:12-19 say about this "quarrel"? ¶ 2

5. What is Screwtape's response to Wormwood on whether he "regards being in love as a desirable state for a human or not?" ¶ 3

6. Screwtape provides a couple of options for exploiting the patient based on whether he is an arrogant or emotional man. The patient's character will determine whether "being in love" is good or bad. Describe those below. ¶ 3

Arrogant Man -

Emotional Man -

7. If neither of those options works, how is Wormwood to steer his patient in regards to marriage? ¶ 3

8. Read 2 Corinthians 6:14. What does it mean to be unequally yoked in marriage? Do you think this is a common occurrence in marriages? How does 1 Corinthians 7:12-13 instruct us to handle this matter?

Answer Guide Available at www.ScrewtapeLettersStudyGuide.com

Notes:

LETTER 20
SEXUAL TASTE

For the time being, the patient has been able to withstand Wormwood's attacks on his chastity. Screwtape suggests that Wormwood try another route: fill the man's thoughts with the idea that chastity is unhealthy. Wormwood can best accomplish this by capitalizing on a particular culture's taste in women as often manipulated by the media. Screwtape says that if they cannot use the man's sexuality to make him unchaste, then using it to find the wrong woman to marry is also desirable.

> *You will find, if you look carefully into any human's heart, that he is haunted by at least two imaginary women—a terrestrial and an infernal Venus, and that his desire differs qualitatively according to its object.* – Screwtape

Discussion Questions

1. Screwtape chastises Wormwood for directly attacking the patient's chastity. Through this attack, what "dangerous truth" did the patient learn about sexual temptation? ¶ 1

2. According to Screwtape, temptation loses its power once God intervenes. What does 1 Corinthians 10:13 say regarding temptation? Why do you think God allows temptations? ¶ 1

3. What is the difference between chastity and abstinence? How can we effectively teach our children the importance of chastity and not just abstinence?

4. What does Screwtape say is a demon's best weapon regarding temptation? ¶ 1

5. According to Screwtape, there is a demonic strategy in twisting "sexual taste" through the ages. He gives reference to past ages and to the current "age of jazz". What do you think is the ideal "sexual taste" for a man or woman in today's culture? How does the media influence what we find desirable? ¶ 3

6. At the end of paragraph 3, we learn that Screwtape seeks to make the "role of the eye in sexuality more and more important." If the role of the eye (physical appearance) in sexuality is exaggerated, what will be its inevitable outcome? Should we discount physical appearance as a part of sexual attraction? ¶ 3

7. Screwtape says that each man loves a terrestrial and infernal Venus. Describe these "two imaginary women" below. How would you describe the male version of each of these "Venus types"? ¶ 4

Terrestrial Venus –

Infernal Venus –

8. Read 1 Corinthians 6:15-20. What does this passage tell us about the effects of sexual sin?

Notes:

LETTER 21
ENTITLEMENT

In this letter, Screwtape explores the concept of how humans relate to the ownership of their time, money, bodies, and souls. Screwtape instructs Wormwood to employ a strategy that encourages the patient to believe that his time is his own, and when unexpected demands encroach on his time, he has the right to become angry, exasperated, and impatient.

> *At present the Enemy says "Mine" of everything on the pedantic, legalistic ground that He made it: Our Father hopes in the end to say "Mine" of all things on the more realistic and dynamic ground of conquest.* – Screwtape

Discussion Questions

1. Why would Screwtape suggest a strategy that involved darkening the patient's intellect prior to moral attack? ¶ 1

2. What does Screwtape mean when he talks about people making claims on their own life? How do you respond when your plans are intruded upon? Why is it hard for us to accept that claims over our lives are not ours to make? ¶ 2

3. Read Mark 5:21-34. In this passage, Jesus is interrupted by a synagogue leader named Jairus who is seeking help for his sick little girl, and then, almost immediately, he is interrupted again by a woman seeking help for a long-term illness. How did Jesus handle these unplanned intrusions on His time?

4. Why did Screwtape say that man assumes he owns his own time and would be relieved if the hardest thing God asked him to do in any given day were to listen "to the conversation of a foolish woman"? ¶ 3

5. Read James 4:13-17. As a Christian, why is having a personal "sense of ownership" of our time "equally funny in Heaven and in Hell?" ¶ 4

6. According to Screwtape, what are some arguments against chastity when considering ownership of our body? In what ways do you see this demonstrated in today's culture?

7. Screwtape manages to go from ownership of "my boot", to "my dog", to "my wife" and eventually to "my God". How can this tendency towards possession be related to the sin of pride and idolatry? ¶ 5

8. Why does Screwtape say the word "Mine" cannot be uttered by a human being about anything? Screwtape hopes to claim victory in the end. How is this different from our hope? ¶ 6

Answer Guide Available at www.ScrewtapeLettersStudyGuide.com

Notes:

LETTER 22
THE CHRISTIAN LIFE

In this letter, Screwtape is obviously annoyed. Wormwood has reported Screwtape to the Secret Police about some "unguarded expressions" in one of his last letters. Screwtape has since smoothed it over but assures Wormwood that he will be dealt with. Even worse, the patient has fallen in love with a Christian woman that Wormwood has failed mentioned in communication with Screwtape.

> *A Noise, the grand dynamism, the audible expression of all that is exultant, ruthless, and virile—Noise which alone defends us from silly qualms, despairing scruples, and impossible desires. We will make the whole universe a noise in the end.* – Screwtape

Discussion Questions

1. How does Screwtape describe the patient's newfound love? Provide as many descriptors as you can find. Why is he so frustrated by her? ¶ 2

2. Screwtape is horrified by what he finds in this girl's dossier (a dossier is a collection of documents about a particular person). If Hell kept a dossier on you, what would Screwtape find? Would he be as upset and frustrated as he is with this girl?

3. Why does Screwtape refer to God as a "hedonist at heart" (one who believes the pursuit of pleasure is the most important thing in life)? What does Screwtape mean by "Everything has to be *twisted before* it's any use to us"? ¶ 3

4. What pleasures does Screwtape mention that humans can do "all day long without His minding in the least"? In today's culture, how do tempters twist pleasures? ¶ 3

5. Why does Screwtape describe the woman's family and home as having an infectious stink? Why does Screwtape say that this is the type of house that "he [the patient] ought to have never entered"? Describe in your own words the experience of being around someone who is so transformed by Christ that their presence makes you feel different? ¶ 4

6. Why do you think that Screwtape hates both music and silence? Read Psalm 46:10. What does this passage say about the importance of silence? ¶ 5

7. Why does Screwtape prefer noise? Think about the noise in your life. How can a noisy environment dull our senses and hinder our abilities to make moral decisions? ¶ 5

8. Screwtape vows, "We will make the whole universe noise in the end." Read 1 Peter 5:8-9. How does Peter's illustration of Satan as a roaring lion and his goal of devouring you keep you aware of the noise and distractions in your life? ¶ 5

9. At the end of the letter, Screwtape becomes so upset that he turns into a centipede. He tries to explain away his temporary transformation as a glorious manifestation. Read 2 Corinthians 5:17. How is the Christian's transformation into a "new creation" different? ¶ 6

Answer Guide Available at www.ScrewtapeLettersStudyGuide.com

Notes:

LETTER 23
THE HISTORICAL JESUS

Wormwood's patient has not only been assimilated into the girl's family, but he has also found a new set of Christian friends. In this letter, Screwtape says that if they cannot remove spirituality from the patient's life, then they must corrupt it. After surveying the patient's new friends, he instructs Wormwood to attack along the two topics we typically like to avoid—politics and religion. He is to create disagreements and confusion.

> *A spoiled saint, a Pharisee, an inquisitor, or a magician, makes better sport in Hell than a mere common tyrant or debauchee.* - Screwtape

Discussion Questions

1. What types of attack have Screwtape and Wormwood used up to this point? How is the new strategy different? Why could this be the most dangerous? ¶ 1

2. Read 2 Corinthians 11:12-15. What does Paul mean by "masquerading as an angel of light"? Read Psalm 119:130. How can we discern which light is from God and which is from Satan?

3. The "historical Jesus" that Screwtape refers to is an attempt by each generation to reinvent Jesus according to the scholarly ideas or theories of that generation. As a result, it changes every 30 years or so. In the prior generation it was promoted along "liberal and humanitarian lines". In the patient's generation, it was being promoted on "Marxian, catastrophic, and revolutionary lines." What is the fashionable teaching about Jesus in our culture today? ¶ 3

4. Screwtape identifies four opportunities where tempters can be successful using the "historical Jesus" theories. What is the first opportunity, and how does it help Screwtape? *(hint: it begins "In the first place")* ¶ 3

5. What is the second opportunity, and how does it help Screwtape? What is wrong with considering Jesus to be nothing more than a great moral teacher? ¶ 3

6. What is the third opportunity, and how does it help Screwtape. ¶ 3

7. What is the fourth opportunity and how does it help Screwtape? ¶ 3

8. It is good for a Christian to be aware of social responsibilities, but why should we also be careful in using Christianity as a means to obtain social justice? ¶ 4

Answer Guide Available at www.ScrewtapeLettersStudyGuide.com

Notes:

LETTER 24
IGNORANCE AN ARROGANCE

In this letter, humility is once again set forth as a major Christian virtue. Having found a small fault in the young woman's worldview (she believes that any belief different from hers is absurd), Screwtape lays plans to set a trap for the man due in part because of his love for the girl. Although this flaw is minor within the girl, Screwtape believes Wormwood may be able to exploit it within the man by causing him to develop real spiritual pride. This is made somewhat easier by the fact that a group of very mature Christians have graciously included him in their inner circle of faith. The patient receives this invitation because of his association with the girl and her family—not because he has earned the right.

> *It is always the novice who exaggerates. The man who has risen in society is over-refined, the young scholar is pedantic. In this new circle your patient is a novice.* – Screwtape

Discussion Questions

1. Through correspondence with Slumtrimpet, the tempter in charge of the girl, what fault did Screwtape find in the girl's character? How did he suggest Wormwood take this minor flaw in the girl and use it against the man? ¶ 1

2. What are some stereotypes that Christians might believe to be true based on what they've been taught? (For example: Christians are happier than people who are not Christians.) At what point in our Christian walk might we be more prone to think of ourselves as superior to non-Christians?

3. Read Philippians 2:3. What is Paul's direction about pride in the presence of others especially non-Christians?

4. In addition to the man being in love with the girl, why else does Screwtape believe he is susceptible to spiritual pride? ¶ 2

5. Why does Screwtape consider spiritual pride to be "the strongest and most beautiful of the vices"? Read Luke 18:9-14. How did Jesus confront such pride in this parable? ¶ 2

6. How does someone who has been raised in a good Christian home and has been soundly indoctrinated with spiritual disciplines such as daily Bible study and prayer avoid spiritual pride?

7. In your own words, describe the Christian circle the man finds himself in? Are you more like the man or the people surrounding him? ¶ 3

8. Screwtape says, "The idea of belonging to an inner ring, of being in a secret, is very sweet to him." Many churches today invest in women's retreats, men's groups, softball leagues, music productions, and facilities while spending only a small percentage of their budget on benevolence, missions, and outreach. Read James 2:1-4. What would James' warning be to these churches?

Answer Guide Available at www.ScrewtapeLettersStudyGuide.com

Notes:

LETTER 25
THE SAME OLD THING

Because humans exist within time, we naturally desire change. In this letter, Screwtape wants Wormwood to capitalize on the patient's natural desire for change. By increasing his fear of "the Same Old Thing", he can be made discontent with his life and eventually his faith. As a result, the patient will become restless in his never-ending search for something new and exciting.

> *The game is to have them running about with fire extinguishers whenever there is a flood, and all crowding to that side of the boat which is already nearly gunwale under.* – Screwtape

Discussion Questions

1. Screwtape is uneasy with the patient's new friends and describes them as being "merely Christian". What does he mean by "merely Christian"? Why would he be concerned? ¶ 1

2. Why would Screwtape want to keep the patient in a state he calls "Christianity And"? What are some examples of fashionable trends being added to Christianity today to keep it fresh? ¶ 1

3. How can the restlessness associated with the "the Same Old Thing" impact and influence our lives? Change may bring temporary satisfaction, but what do we do when the novelty wears off? ¶ 2

4. Why do we have such a desire for change? How does the creation story in Genesis 1 introduce change? How did God balance out our desire for change? ¶ 2

5. What is the connection Screwtape makes between gluttony and a desire for change? ¶ 3

6. The law of diminishing returns states that there is a point in production where with every additional unit of input added, there will be smaller increases in the amount of output—with all other variables remaining the same. How does this law apply to increasing desires and diminishing pleasures? ¶ 4

7. Read 1 Timothy 6:6-11 and Philippians 4:11-13. What does Paul tell us about living with contentment in these two passages? How is contentment ultimately a heart change?

8. What three questions does Screwtape not want men to ask about issues and decisions? What questions would he rather men ask? What's wrong with asking if an idea is relevant rather than asking if it is prudent or true? ¶ 6

Notes:

LETTER 26
UNSELFISHNESS

In this letter, Screwtape talks about the difference between unselfishness and charity. He suggests Wormwood sow seeds of unselfishness during the patient's courtship in hopes of causing marital discord later in life. Since the two are enchanted in the early days of natural attraction, they are putting their best foot forward in order to hide any weakness. However, after the honeymoon phase ends and the *real* marriage begins, each will start expecting the other to maintain their unselfishness which neither of them will be able to do.

> *...teach a man to surrender benefits not that others may be happy in having them but that he may be unselfish in forgoing them.* – Screwtape

Discussion Questions

1. Screwtape says, "courtship is the time for sowing those seeds which will grow up ten years later into domestic hatred." What are some things that couples might do for each other during courtship that they fail to do in marriage? ¶ 1

2. The definition of enchantment is the state of being under a spell or a feeling of great pleasure or delight—in the case of the patient an enchantment of love. Why would Screwtape want these enchanted lovebirds to be deceived into thinking that any problem they will encounter is solved simply because they are in love? ¶ 1

3. God created us to experience and enjoy both eros and agape love. Read Song of Solomon 1:1-4 where eros is used for love and Romans 5:8 where agape is used for love. What is the difference between the two forms of love? Why are each important to the marriage relationship?

4. What is the difference between "unselfishness" and "charity"? Why would Screwtape want to substitute one for the other? ¶ 2

a. Unselfishness –

b. Charity –

5. How does Screwtape say the word "Unselfishness" differs for men and women? Do you agree with his assessment? ¶ 2

a. Women –

b. Men –

6. Screwtape says that we often compete with others to see who can be the most "unselfish". Why would we do this? ¶ 2

7. What does Screwtape mean when he says the couple will be, "mistaking sexual excitement for charity and of thinking that the excitement will last"? ¶ 3

8. Describe the game that Screwtape likes to play called the "Generous Conflict Illusion"? ¶ 4

9. Why does Screwtape not want the couple to notice that, "love is not enough, that charity is needed and not yet achieved and that no external law can supply its place"? What does Luke 6:35 tell us about loving our enemies? ¶ 5

Answer Guide Available at www.ScrewtapeLettersStudyGuide.com

Notes:

LETTER 27
ANSWERS

Wormwood has failed. As the patient's love for the girl continues to grow stronger and war efforts loom, his prayers have shifted from normal "daily bread" prayers to attentive appeals directly to God for guidance. Since Satan is a master at distraction, Screwtape instructs Wormwood to attack the legitimacy of prayer. If he cannot create in the man a pious prayer life, then the next best thing is to convince him that the answers to his prayers are what is going to happen or not happen anyway. If successful, Wormwood might be able to convince the man to stop praying altogether.

> *Don't forget to use the "heads I win, tails you lose" argument. If the thing he prays for doesn't happen, then that is one more proof that petitionary prayers don't work; if it does happen, he will, of course, be able to see some of the physical causes which led up to it, and "therefore it would have happened anyway..."* – Screwtape

Discussion Questions

1. According to Screwtape, what can happen when distractions or sins surface during prayer? What specifically should Wormwood do when distractions or sins surface during the patient's prayers? ¶ 1

2. Read Matthew 6:5-6. What does Jesus say about the "false spirituality" of the Pharisees prayers? Why would the devil want to encourage a sense of "false spirituality" rather than letting you petition God with sincere prayers and questions? ¶ 2

3. Read the Lord's Prayer in Matthew 6:9-13. In your own words, how does Jesus instruct us to pray? How hard is it for you to model this prayer in your daily life?

4. Due to the man's spiritual obedience, Wormwood's efforts to encourage this "false spirituality" will probably not work. What other tactics does Screwtape recommend to steer the patient away from prayer? ¶ 3

5. Describe Screwtape's "heads I win, tails you lose" argument? How can being too focused on the results of prayer actually hinder our prayer life? ¶ 3

6. Read Revelations 22:13. What is the human perspective of time? According to this verse, what is the perspective of time for God? How does this impact your prayer life? ¶ 4

7. Read John 14:13; 15:16; and 16:23. How do we reconcile these verses with statements like, "If God is going to do what He wants, why pray?" or "Why doesn't God seem to answer my prayers?" or "How do I know that what I prayed for wouldn't have happened anyway?" ¶ 4

8. What is "the Historical Point of View"? How does this view actually prevent humans from learning? ¶ 5

Answer Guide Available at www.ScrewtapeLettersStudyGuide.com

Notes:

LETTER 28
PERSEVERANCE

Wormwood's failures keep mounting. The demon was unable to entangle the patient with worldly friends. The patient has fallen in love with a dedicated Christian woman, and none of the attacks on his spiritual life are working at the present. To top it off, Wormwood is showing too much enthusiasm over the potential for human fatalities due to war. Since the patient is a Christian, his death is the last thing that Screwtape wants. In fact, Screwtape says that they must guard the patient's life in order to let real worldliness take root and grow into his middle-age years.

> *They, of course, do tend to regard death as the prime evil and survival as the greatest good. But that is because we have taught them to do so.* – Screwtape

Discussion Questions

1. It seems strange that demons would actually want to keep us safe! Why does Screwtape want to avoid the patient's death at this point in his life? ¶ 1

2. Wormwood assumed the war would have a negative effect on the patient's spiritual life, but it has actually proven to be the opposite. How so? ¶ 1

3. Screwtape said, "Do not let us be infected by our own propaganda." What is the propaganda that he is referring to? How does Philippians 1:21 counter that argument? ¶ 1

4. Screwtape discloses that only if the man is kept alive, will Wormwood have the opportunity to attack him in the middle-age years. What advantage does Screwtape foresee for this period of the man's life?

5. Screwtape suggests attacking the man through either adversity or prosperity in his middle-age years. How are each different? Which of these temptations would be fertile ground for you?

Adversity –

Prosperity –

6. Read 2 Timothy 4:7 and Philippians 3:12-16. What does the Bible say about finishing well? ¶ 1

7. Screwtape says that while we are young, it is hard to keep humans ignorant of religion because of the fascination with music, poetry, love, songbirds, or a sunset. In contrast, as we grow older, what does Screwape say that we steadily apply ourselves toward? Do you agree? ¶ 2

8. Why would Screwtape want us to believe that this world can be turned into heaven? ¶ 2

Answer Guide Available at www.ScrewtapeLettersStudyGuide.com

Notes:

LETTER 29
COWARDICE

In this letter, Screwtape revisits an old topic—fear. This time the context of the war and recent bombings is in the patient's hometown. Screwtape recommends defeating the patient's courage and making him a coward. Since human beings normally feel shame and guilt over cowardice, Screwtape believes that his fear will undermine his courage and drive him away from God.

> *This, indeed, is probably one of the Enemy's motives for creating a dangerous world—a world in which moral issues really come to the point.* – Screwtape

Discussion Questions

1. What is the one thing that Hell's Research Department has not been able to produce? Why are they incapable of doing so? How does knowing that tempters have limitation impact your spiritual life? ¶ 2

2. Screwtape says, "Hatred is best combined with Fear" and "Hatred has its pleasures." How does Screwtape link hatred to fear? Why is hatred and "anodyne for shame"? ¶ 4

3. Read Psalm 27:1, 1 John 4:18; 2 Timothy 1:7. What do these Scripture passages say about fear?

4. Screwtape claims that they have been able to make men proud of most vices, but not of cowardice. Why? What is the danger in inducing patients with cowardice? ¶ 5

5. What does Screwtape say is the formation point of all virtues? Explain what Screwtape means by this. As an example, how was Pilate merciful until it became risky (John 18, 19)? ¶ 6

6. Screwtape's other option is to heap shame on a coward until they break and give in to utter despair. What does despair cause one to do? How did Pilate demonstrate his own despair and cowardice in Matthew 27:24? ¶ 7

7. Read Matthew 16:25. What does Jesus say about the courage necessary to follow him?

8. What does Screwtape mean by, "the emotion of fear is, in itself, no sin and, though we enjoy it, does us no good"? ¶ 8

Notes:

LETTER 30
FATIGUE

Wormwood has been an utter failure. Screwtape not only scolds Wormwood for his incompetence but threatens his very existence as well. The patient is frightened and thinks himself a coward, but he has behaved well during an air raid on his town. He did everything demanded of him and more. However, war can wear you down, and Screwtape instructs Wormwood to capitalize on the man's fatigue in hopes of weakening his resolve. In addition, he tells him to manipulate the man's emotions with the word "real".

> *Whatever men expect they soon come to think they have a right to: the Sense of disappointment can, with very little skill on our part, be turned into a sense of injury.* – Screwtape

Discussion Questions

1. Read Luke 21:12-19. Compare the difference in the way Satan treats his demons to the way God treats His disciples. What is the relationship based on? ¶ 1

2 What does Screwtape say that fatigue and unexpected demands can produce? Provide an example of a time when a "sense of disappointment" turned into a "sense of injury" in your own life? ¶ 2

3. To produce the best results from fatigue, Screwtape says he needs to feed the man false hopes. What false hopes does Screwtape want Wormwood to feed to the man? How can false hopes be a danger to us in our Christian walk? ¶ 2

4. Read Hebrews 11:1. How does the hope Paul describes in this passage differ from the false hope that the world promises?

5. Screwtape admits that demons are comforted when they see us blow our top. Read Romans 5:3-5. What spiritual principal do we need to produce when we are fatigued and angered? Why is it important? ¶ 2

6. According to Screwtape, if a demon cannot make an intellectual attack on the patient's faith, what should he attack? Why is an emotional battle often an easier way for Satan to attack than an intellectual battle—especially when a man is fatigued? ¶ 4

7. What are the two ways in which humans use the word "real"? What example was provided for each? ¶ 4

a.

b.

8. How can Wormwood use these two applications to raise doubts about his patient's faith and persuade him to deny reality? ¶ 4

Answer Guide Available at www.ScrewtapeLettersStudyGuide.com

Notes:

LETTER 31
THE OTHER SIDE

Wormwood has come begging his uncle for compassion after letting his patient escape safely into Heaven. In this last letter, Screwtape is unsympathetic and furious with his nephew as he hates to see "human vermin" be cleansed by the blood of Christ. In no uncertain terms, Screwtape assures Wormwood that he is the stronger of the two demons, and now that the patient has been lost to the Enemy, he promises Wormwood there will be hell to pay.

> *There was a sudden clearing of his eyes (was there not?) as he saw you*
> *for the first time, and recognised the part you had had in him and knew that*
> *you had it no longer. –* Screwtape

Discussion Questions

1. What, ultimately, happens to the patient? ¶s 2 and 3

2. How would you describe the patient's "sudden clearing of the eyes" as he saw Wormwood for the first time on the other side of death? Have you ever experienced "a sudden clearing of the eyes" in some way? What did you gain as a result of that experience? ¶ 2

3. The man died a horrific death, but Screwtape seems to suggest that the man got off relatively easy. How so? ¶ 3

4. What sort of sensory descriptions or insights did the man experience in the aftermath of dying? ¶ 5

5. Read the following verses Job 19:25-27 and 1 Corinthians 15:50-57. What do these verses say about our experience with death?

6. Screwtape says to Wormwood, "As he saw you, he also saw Them." Who is the "Them" and how did the patient respond to them? ¶ 4

7. Who else did the man see upon death? How was being in the presence of God different for both the man and Wormwood? ¶ 5

8. Since the beginning of the book, Screwtape has signed each of his letters as "Your affectionate uncle". Why does he sign off his last letter with "Your increasingly and ravenously affectionate uncle"? ¶ 5

Answer Guide Available at www.ScrewtapeLettersStudyGuide.com

Notes:

QUOTES

All of C.S. Lewis' writings are extremely quotable. In fact, if you search the web you will find plenty of them including websites, Facebook pages, and Twitter feeds dedicated to the task. On the next several pages, you will find some of my favorite quotes from *The Screwtape Letters*. I'm sure you have your own!

LETTER 1

"Teach him to call it 'real life' and don't let him ask what he means by 'real.'" (p. 2)

LETTER 2

"Do not misunderstand me. I do not mean the Church as we see her spread out through all time and space and rooted in eternity, terrible as an army with banners. That, I confess, is a spectacle which makes our boldest tempters uneasy." (p. 5)

"The Enemy allows this disappointment to occur on the threshold of every human endeavor... In every department of life it marks the transition from dreaming aspiration to laborious doing... Desiring their freedom, He therefore refuses to carry them, by their mere affections and habits, to any of the goals which He sets before them: He leaves them to 'do it on their own." (p. 7)

LETTER 3

"Aggravate that most useful human characteristic, the horror and neglect of the obvious." (p. 11-12)

LETTER 4

"It is funny how mortals always picture us as putting things into their minds: in reality our best work is done by keeping things out." (p. 16)

"If he ever consciously directs his prayer 'Not to what I think thou art but to what thou knowest thyself to be', our situation is, for the moment, desperate." (p. 18)

LETTER 5

"When I see the temporal suffering of humans who finally escape us, I feel as if I had been allowed to taste the first course of a rich banquet and then denied the rest. It is worse than not to have tasted it at all." (p. 22)

LETTER 6

"The great thing is to direct the malice to his immediate neighbors whom he meets every day and to thrust his benevolence out to the remote circumference, to people he does not know. The malice thus becomes wholly real and the benevolence largely imaginary." (p. 28)

"Of all humans the English are in this respect the most deplorable milksops. They are creatures of that miserable sort who loudly proclaim that torture is too good for their enemies and then give tea and cigarettes to the first wounded German pilot who turns up at the back door." (p. 17)

LETTER 7

"All extremes, except extreme devotion to the Enemy, are to be encouraged." (p. 32)

LETTER 8

"He wants them to learn to walk and must therefore take away His hand; and if only the will to walk is really there He is pleased even with their stumbles." (p. 40)

"Our cause is never more in danger than when a human, no longer desiring, but still intending, to do our Enemy's will, looks round upon a universe from which every trace of Him seems to have vanished, and asks why he has been forsaken, and still obeys." (p. 40)

"One must face the fact that all the talk about His love for men, and His service being perfect freedom, is not (as one would gladly believe) mere propaganda, but an appalling truth. He really does want to fill the universe with a lot of loathsome little replicas of Himself." (pp. 38-39)

LETTER 9

"I know we have won many a soul through pleasure. All the same, it is His invention, not ours. He made the pleasures: all our research so far has not enabled us to produce one. All we can do is to encourage the humans to take the pleasures which our Enemy has produced, at times, or in ways, or in degrees, which He has forbidden." (p. 44)

LETTER 10

"All mortals tend to turn into the thing they are pretending to be." (p. 50)

"I see few of the old warnings about Worldly Vanities, the Choice of Friends, and the Value of Time. All that, your patient would probably classify as 'Puritanism'—and may I remark in passing that the value we have given to that word is one of the really solid triumphs of the last hundred years? By it we rescue annually thousands of humans from temperance, chastity, and sobriety of life." (p. 51)

LETTER 11

"Fun is closely related to Joy - a sort of emotional froth arising from the play instinct. It is very little use to us. It can sometimes be used, of course, to divert humans from something else which the Enemy would like them to be feeling or doing: but in itself it has wholly undesirable tendencies; it promotes charity, courage, contentment, and many other evils." (p. 54)

"Among flippant people the Joke is always assumed to have been made. No one actually makes it; but every serious subject is discussed in a manner which implies that they have already found a ridiculous side to it... It [flippancy] is a thousand miles away from joy: it deadens, instead of sharpening, the intellect; and it excites no affection between those who practise it." (p. 56)

LETTER 12

"One of my own patients said on his arrival down here, 'I now see that I spent most of my life in doing neither what I ought nor what I liked.'" (p. 60)

"Indeed the safest road to Hell is the gradual one—the gentle slope, soft underfoot, without sudden turnings, without milestones, without signposts." (p. 61)

"Nothing is very strong: strong enough to steal away a man's best years not in sweet sins but in a dreary flickering of the mind over it knows not what and knows not why, in the gratification of curiosities so feeble that the man is only half aware of them, in drumming of fingers and kicking of heels, in whistling tunes that he does not like, or in long, dim labyrinth of reveries that have not even lust or ambition to give them a relish, but which, once association has started them, the creature is too weak and fuddled to shake off." (p. 60)

LETTER 13

"The characteristic of Pains and Pleasures is that they are unmistakably real, and therefore, as far as they go, give the man who feels them a touchstone of reality." (p. 64)

"When He talks of their losing their selves, He only means abandoning the clamour of self-will; once they have done that, He really gives them back all their personality, and boasts (I am afraid, sincerely) that when they are wholly His they will be more themselves than ever. Hence, while He is delighted to see them sacrificing even their innocent wills to His, He hates to see them drifting away from their own nature for any other reason." (p. 65)

"The man who truly and disinterestedly enjoys any one thing in the world, for its own sake, and without caring two-pence what other people say about it, is by that very fact forearmed against some of our subtlest modes of attack." (p. 66)

"Let him do anything but act. No amount of piety in his imagination and affections will harm us if we can keep it out of his will... Active habits are strengthened by repetition but passive ones are weakened. The more often he feels without acting, the less he will be able ever to act, and, in the long run, the less he will be able to feel." (p. 67)

LETTER 14

"The Enemy wants him, in the end, to be so free from any bias in his own favour that he can rejoice in his own talents as frankly and gratefully as in his neighbour's talents." (p. 71)

"For we must never forget what is the most repellent and inexplicable trait in our Enemy; He *really* loves the hairless bipeds He has created and always gives back to them with His right hand what He has taken away with His left." (p. 72)

"Even of his sins the Enemy does not want him to think too much: once they are repented, the sooner the man turns his attention outward, the better the Enemy is pleased." (p. 73)

LETTER 15

"In a word, the Future is, of all things, the thing least like eternity. It is the most completely temporal part of time - for the Past is frozen and no longer flows, and the Present is all lit up with eternal rays... Hence nearly all vices are rooted in the future. Gratitude looks to the past and love to the present; fear, avarice, lust, and ambition look ahead." (p. 76)

"It is far better to make them live in the Future. Biological necessity makes all their passions point in that direction already, so that thought about the Future inflames hope and fear. Also, it is unknown to them, so that in making them think about it we make them think of unrealities." (p. 76)

"The duty of planning the morrow's work is *today's* duty; though its material is borrowed from the future, the duty, like all duties, is in the Present." (p. 77)

LETTER 16

"The real fun is working up hatred between those who say 'mass' and those who say 'holy communion' when neither party could possibly state the difference between, say, Hooker's doctrine and Thomas Aquinas', in any form which would hold water for five minutes." (p. 84)

LETTER 17

"Because what she wants is smaller and less costly than what has been set before her, she never recognizes as gluttony her determination to get what she wants, however troublesome it may be to others... She never finds any servant or any friend who can do these simple things 'properly' - because her 'properly' conceals and insatiable demand for the exact, and almost impossible, palatal pleasures which she imagines she remembers from the past; a past described by her as 'the days when you could get good servants' but known to us as the days when her senses were more easily please and she had pleasures of other kinds which made her less dependent on those of the table." (pp. 88-89)

LETTER 18

"We have done this through the poets and novelists by persuading humans that a curious, and usually short-lived, experience which they call 'being in love' is the only respectable ground for marriage; that marriage can, and out to, render this excitement permanent; and that a marriage which does not do so is no longer binding. This idea is our parody of an idea that came from the Enemy." (p. 93)

"Thus He is not content, even Himself, to be a sheer arithmetical unity; He claims to be three as well as one, in order that this nonsense about Love may find a foothold in His own nature." (p. 94)

"Now comes the joke. The Enemy described a married couple as 'one flesh'. He did not say ' a happily married couple' or 'a couple who married because they were in love', but you can make the humans ignore that." (p. 95)

"The truth is that wherever a man lies with a woman, there, whether they like it or not, a transcendental relation is set up between them which must be eternally enjoyed or eternally

114

endured." (p. 96)

LETTER 19

"And there lies the great task. We know that He cannot really love: nobody can: it doesn't make sense. If we could only find out what He is really up to!" (p. 101)

LETTER 20

"It is the business of these great masters to produce at every age a general misdirection of what may be called sexual 'taste'. This they do by working through the small circle of popular artists, dressmakers, actresses and advertisers who determine the fashionable type. The aim is to guide each sex away from those members of the other with whom spiritually helpful, happy, and fertile marriages are most likely." (p. 106)

LETTER 21

"Men are not angered by mere misfortune but by misfortune conceived as injury." (p. 111)

"The man can neither make, nor retain, one moment of time; it all comes to him by pure gift; he might as well regard the sun and moon as his chattels." (p. 112)

"Much of the modern resistance to chastity comes from men's beliefs that they 'own' their bodies—those vast and perilous estates, pulsating with the energy that made the worlds, in which they find themselves without their consent and from which they are ejected at the pleasure of Another!" (p. 113)

"In the long run either Our Father or the Enemy will say 'Mine' of each thing that exists, and specially of each man. They will find out in the end, never fear, to whom their time, their souls, and their bodies really belong—certainly not to them, whatever happens," (pp. 114-115).

LETTER 22

"He has a bourgeois mind. he has filled His world full of pleasures. There are things for humans to do all day long without His minding in the least—sleeping, washing, eating, drinking, making love, playing, praying, working. Everything has to be twisted before it's any use to us. We fight under cruel disadvantages. Nothing is naturally on our side." (p. 118)

"He's a hedonist at heart. All those fasts and vigils and stakes and crosses are only a facade. Or only like foam on the seashore. Out at sea, out in His sea, there is pleasure and more pleasure. He makes no secret of it; at His right hand are 'pleasures forevermore.' Ugh! I don't think He has the least inkling of that high and austere mystery to which we rise in the Miserific Vision. He's vulgar, Wormwood. He has a bourgeois mind." (p. 118)

LETTER 23

"Distract men's minds from who He is, and what He did. We first make Him solely a teacher, and then conceal the very substantial agreement between His teachings and those of all other great moral teachers. For humans must not be allowed to notice that all great moralists are sent by the Enemy not to inform men but to remind them, to restate the primeval moral platitudes against our continual concealment of them." (p. 125)

"Men or nations who think they can revive the Faith in order to make a good society might just as well think they can use the stairs of Heaven as a short cut to the nearest chemist's shop... You see the rift? 'Believe this, not because it is true, but for some other reason.' That's the game." (p. 127)

LETTER 24

"You must teach him to mistake this contrast between the circle that delights and the circle that bores him for the contrast between Christians and unbelievers." (p. 132)

LETTER 25

"If they must be Christians let them at least be Christians with a difference. Substitute for the faith itself some Fashion with a Christian colouring." (p. 135)

"He has balanced the love of change in them by a love of permanence. He has contrived to gratify both tastes together in the very world He has made, by that union of change and permanence which we call Rhythm. he gives them the seasons, each season different yet every year the same, so that spring is always felt as a novelty yet always as the recurrence of an immemorial theme." (p. 136)

"The pleasure of novelty is by its very nature more subject than any other to the law of diminishing returns." (p. 137)

"Once they knew that some changes were for the better, and others for the words, and others again indifferent. We have largely removed this knowledge...We have trained them to think of the Future as a promised land which favoured heroes attain - not as something which everyone reaches at the rate of sixty minutes an hour, whatever he does, whoever he is." (p. 139)

LETTER 26

"The grand problem is that of 'Unselfishness'... Teach a man to surrender benefits not that others may be happy in having them but that he may be unselfish in forgoing them." (p. 141)

"They are under the double blindness of mistaking sexual excitement for charity and of thinking that the excitement will last." (p. 143)

LETTER 27

"On the seemingly pious ground that 'praise and communion with God is the true prayer', humans can often be lured into direct disobedience to the Enemy who...has definitely told them to pray for their daily bread and the recovery of their sick." (p. 148)

"Only the learned read old books and we have now so dealt with the learned that they are of all men the least likely to acquire wisdom by doing so." (p. 150)

"Since we cannot deceive the whole human race all the time, it is most important thus to cut every generation off from all others; for where learning makes a free commerce between the ages there is always the danger that the characteristic errors of one may be corrected by the characteristic truths of another." (p. 151)

LETTER 28

"The truth is that the Enemy, having oddly destined these mere animals to life in His own eternal world, has guarded them pretty effectively from the danger of feeling at home anywhere else." (pp. 155-156)

"Experience, in the peculiar sense we teach them to give it, is, by the by, a most useful word. A great human philosopher nearly let our secret out when he said that where Virtue is concerned 'Experience is the most of illusion'..." (p. 156)

LETTER 29

"We have made men proud of most vices, but not of cowardice." (p. 160)

"This, indeed, is probably one of the Enemy's motives for creating a dangerous world-a world in which moral issues really come to the point. he sees as well as you do that courage is not simply one of the virtues, but the form of every virtue at the testing point, which means, at the point of highest reality... It is therefore possible to lose as much as we gain by making your man a coward; he may learn too much about himself!" (pp. 161-162)

"For remember, the act of cowardice is all that matters; the emotion of fear is, in itself, no sin..." (p. 163)

LETTER 30

"Fatigue can produce extreme gentleness, and quiet of mind, and even something like vision." (p. 166)

"In this, as in the problem of cowardice, the thing to avoid is the total commitment. Whatever he says, let his inner resolution be not to bear whatever comes to him, but to bear it 'for a reasonable period'- and let the reasonable period be shorter than the trial is likely to last." (p. 167)

"The creatures are always accusing one another of wanting 'to eat the cake and have it'; but thanks to our labours they are more often in the predicament of paying for the cake and not eating it." (p. 169)

LETTER 31

"He had no faintest conception till that very hour of how they would look, and even doubted their existence. But when he saw them he knew that he had always known them and realised what part each one of them had played at many an hour in his life when he had supposed himself alone, so that now he could say to them, one by one, not 'Who are you?' but 'So it was you all the time.'" (pp. 173-174)

"Pain he may still have to encounter, but they embrace those pains. They would not barter them for any earthly pleasure." (p. 174)

MERE CHRISTIANITY STUDY GUIDE

A Bible Study on the
C.S. Lewis Book Mere Christianity

By Steven Urban

Mere Christianity Study Guide takes participants through a study of C.S. Lewis's classic, Mere Christianity. Yet despite its recognition as a "classic," there is surprisingly little available today in terms of a serious study course.

This 12-week Bible study digs deep into each chapter and in turn into Lewis's thoughts. Perfect for small group sessions this interactive workbook includes daily, individual study as well as a complete appendix and commentary to supplement and further clarify certain topics. Multiple week format options are also included.

The Mere Christianity Study Guide features:
- 12 Week Bible study with multiple week options included
- Interactive Workbook with daily study
- Complete appendix for commentary and to go deeper
- Study questions are ideal for group discussion
- Answers to all questions included online
- Ideal for small groups or individual study

I recommend the book for all who take their faith seriously and want to grow to be all they can be in Christ. **Jerry Root PhD, Editor of The Quotable C.S. Lewis, Consulting Editor of The C.S. Lewis Study Bible**

Available at Amazon

Learn More at www.MereChristianity.org

Made in the USA
Monee, IL
29 January 2024

52578474R00072